The Hungry Ghost Diner

Kelly Ann Ellis

The Hungry Ghost Diner

Kelly Ann Ellis

LITERARY PRESS
LAMAR UNIVERSITY

ISBN: 978-1-942956-99-0
LOC: 2023939112
Cover Concept: James Ellis

Lamar University Literary Press
Beaumont, TX

Acknowledgments

Thank you to the editors of these publications where my poems
have previously appeared

di-verse-city, Anthology of Austin International Poetry Festival
Boundless, Anthology of Rio Grande Valley International Poetry
Festival
Houston Poetry Fest anthology
Ilya's Honey
Friendswood Library Ekphrastic Poetry Anthology 2022
Wingless Dreamer
The Houston Chronicle
The San Antonio Express News

Recent Poetry from Lamar University Literary Press

Lisa Adams, *Xuai*
Walter Bargen, *My Other Mother's Red Mercedes*
Christine Boldt, *In Every Tatter*
Devan Burton, *A Room for Us*
Jerry Bradley, *Collapsing into Possibility*
Mark Busby, *Through Our Times*
Julie Chappell, *Mad Habits of a Life*
Stan Crawford, *Resisting Gravity*
Glover Davis, *Academy of Dreams*
William Virgil Davis, *The Bones Poems*
Chris Ellery, *Elder Tree*
Dede Fox, *On Wings of Silence*
Alan Gann, *That's Entertainment*
Larry Griffin, *Cedar Plums*
Michelle Hartman, *Irony and Irrelevance*
Lynn Hoggard, *First Light*
Michael Jennings, *Crossings: A Record of Travel*
Gretchen Johnson, *A Trip Through Downer, Minnesota*
Markham Johnson, *Dear Dreamland*
Betsy Joseph & Chip Dameron, *Relatively Speaking*
Ulf Kirchdorfer, *Chewing Green Leaves*
Jim McGarrah, *A Balancing Act*
J. Pittman McGehee, *Nod of Knowing*
Laurence Musgrove, *Bluebonnet Sutras*
Benjamin Myers, *The Family Book of Martyrs*
Janice Northerns, *Some Electric Hum*
Godspower Oboido, *Wandering Feet on Pebbled Shores*
Carol Coffee Reposa, *Sailing West*
Jan Seale, *Particulars*
Steven Schroeder, *the moon, not the finger, pointing*
Glen Sorestad, *Hazards of Eden*
Vincent Spina, *The Sumptuous Hills of Gulfport*
W.K. Stratton, *Betrayal Creek*
Wally Swist, *Invocation*
Ken Waldman, *Sports Page*
Loretta Diane Walker, *Ode to My Mother's Voice*
Dan Williams, *At the Gates, a Refuge of Milkweed and Sunflowers*
Jonas Zdanys, *The Angled Road*

For information on these and other Lamar University Literary
Press books go to www.Lamar.edu/literarypress

CONTENTS

Late Night

Open for Business

Greasy Spoon

Post-Church Lunch

Crooked Mile Café

Late Night

Strings

Inspired by Mangbetu anthropomorphic harp, Museum of Fine Arts Houston

Ghosts are the worst addicts. It wasn't wine
or women but song that strung me out and along
all my life, this harp the opium pipe, my name a graven
love-mark on its neck.

And yes, there was one siren whose aria hummed
in my blood. Where she was, tunes bloomed.
I forget her name, strange, can't retrace the contours
of her face, the way she wore her chignon, the curve
of her bosom—was she one or many women?

Musicians play for ladies; they are a reason for music
but not the only. Melody is not needy, rewards richly,
a seasoned paramour, no virgin of tears and demands,
sweet of tongue and hands, beholden.

What instrument? Was it God in my palm who painted
me golden? Women, religion, heaven—one time, all mine.
This harp houses a legion of seraphs and demons. Listen!
They strain to strum the names they lost, beckon lovers
they can't recall. Only their fingers remember
these strings.

Last Tryst

Legend has it, Houdini told his wife he would meet her
in Galveston at the Martini Bar every New Year's Eve
for a tryst in the afterlife. She should wear that crimson dress,
chinchilla cape, turned down hose, and those shoes, the ones
that made her taller than him. When he died, the plan played on:
Champagne corks orbited the sun, Texas swings were swung,
rugs got cut. The deep sweet kiss at midnight, as always, a must.

Then one year she stood him up.

He knew in his bones she must be dead, too, but where? Neither
here nor there. So he started knocking on stones, storm-surging
the cemetery on Broadway, where folks hold their breath for at least
two blocks lest their souls get snatched—a graveyard swept away
every hundred years or so by a hurricane wearing a woman's name.

That year was a hurricane year, weather freakish, and it snowed.
Even the beaches were white that night, and those overgrown
graves shone like ghosts. Houdini howled himself a blue norther,
cut such a ruckus that he woke the dead, who curtly said that he,
of all folks, should have shook them chains years ago. Rattled,
he raged and ranged—some knots not so easily slipped.

Then he slid into a drift. That's when he saw white.

This is it, he thought, same old tunnel of light. Then her red dress—
not his life—flashed before his eyes. She glowed like the last drag
of the best cigarette. He felt the frost go gold, nuzzled her shoes,
shimmied off her hose, buried his head in her soft, sweet lap. She
folded in to kiss him, stoking just enough fire to warm them both
one last time.

What her Paintings Said at her Well-Attended Wake

The sea witch said, I was never a witch. She called me
that because of my claws, my pointed face, the way waves
lapped my lap. Now that she's dead, I want to set the matter
straight: I am the artist's wife. She met me when she bought me,
noted my big breasts. But no matter the medium, she saw herself.

The resemblance is uncanny. How she hated her body.

The tree said, I know I am disproportionate, monstrous, twice
the size of the house I shade, white, where three people stroll
in front, again, too large, half the size of the house. The green coat
is Grandmother; blue, Brother. The pink frock, of course, a girl. Her.
All her, even the sea witch who is not a witch. Her grandmother made
me, so *she* saved me. Loved ghosts more than she ever loved the living.

Four children with three different fathers. Why the house is so small.

The picket fence on fire said, I am not on fire. That is a geranium
flanked by an azalea, and a woman with crimson hair kissing a sailor.
Painted by her daughter at fifteen, I was deemed by owner to mean
the demise of her picket fence dream. A tree towers over this mess,
branches bare. The paint has started to flake, like bark, and this tree
is her marriage, and of course, her. Everywhere. She is everything.

Especially the woman submerged in a field of sunflowers that are not
sunflowers but the place she set her purse down when the officer said,
Step out of the car and the oil fields glittered like the magic ice castles
she leaned toward but could not reach because of branches that are cages.
The real canvas is her scarlet dress. Velvet. You can tell if you touch it.

Poem for Dali's *Dream Caused by the Flight of a Bee around a Pomegranate a Second Before Awakening*

Take me, I am the drug—
pit of this unruly fruit
before the bloom.

Seas spout, rocks float
koi catches fire
tigers soar

out of the knot—
ruby pearls unstrung
virgin flesh yet taut

unstung, adrift
in a blue ocean.
Sleep is a tethered elephant,

balloon of oblivion
and I, the drug,
stay the sting

aimed at arms
unarmed.
I am

hoarder of orchards
keeper of bees
trapper of atoms

unsprung.

I am the drug
dissolving beneath
your tongue.

She Passed with Flying Colors

After untitled installation *by Joel Shapiro, Rice University*

She met her fate, the Dancing Queen,
that Mardi Gras float beloved by Abba fans
and disco revelers, on Fat Tuesday. A besotted blues
artist, commandeering a street repair vehicle wailed
I'm a steamroller baby, gonna roll right over you and did.

Maybe some old pagan entity staged a coup,
likely Neptune, upset about Lent impending.
Regardless, magic ensued. Some of the beads
fluttered, flatter than flitters, trailing strings
untethered, floating off from the Big Bang,
if not to a better place, at least another life,
possessed of newfound purpose and delusions:

The yellow claimed to be a lifeboat floating
sunflowers in ice buckets from the Titanic.
The red said it was a door, portal to that place
where rivers run blood and bloated frogs croak
the Ten Commandments in jaded cacophony.

The purple purported to be the box that Pandora
crawled into to hide from the havoc.
The tan, claiming to be a coffin, posted its profile
on Tinder with the descriptor, slender.

The pink became a plank and took me on a walk
over misty, monstered abysses of murk and words.
The orange insisted it was a seesaw I could ride
with my imaginary friend. I see said I. You saw said he.
Doomed to discord, we were in love with possibility.

The nondescript beads became faded beams
to and from nothing, weeping, Wherever you go
there you are. The dead are stars, I'm told.
Stars, exploding in chaos and color, create
a vortex, suspended like the moments that froze,
occasioning matter. Then they recede, retrace,
retract their steps—parade over, streets swept.

Les Fauves

Outside this spirit house
the saffron sky
sets fire
to silk left in the sun.
Orchids arch toward warmth.
Locusts swarm.

Is this the incense
abandoned at my temple?
Dominoes, Tarot
Salem Lights
a Diet Coke—

Daylight's a vise.

Inside the bloated afternoon
ghosts give it a go
renounce their holiest of holies
trade paradise
for a glut, a fuck
another throw
of the dice
one last
drag.

Swollen then sated
the day dissipates
collapses the color
of fever.

Three Dreams

I

Manatees with wings and snub pig noses
in what might be any city mount the air, ungainly,
plop down in rush hour sludge. I nudge a big one
with my Buick. It climbs, then nose-dives into traffic.
Commuters panic, abandon cars, leap off the bridge,
ties flying, stilettos akimbo. But the bridge is not high
like the Golden Gate or Brooklyn or even St. John's.
Folks jump with their briefcases clutched, recover dignity,
hurry off unflustered to the city, leaving me me me
to tend the manatees.

II

A spot forms on my lip. It is big, the size of a grape,
and it oozes. I don't know what it is. Does he see?
Can I kiss him? Must I tell? It crusts like nothing much,
collapses, and fear falls into the crater the spot leaves.
Terror drains into my brain. I see his name everywhere:
mixed in my email, coffee, wine, granola, greasy enchiladas.
I'm inherently unhealthy. I don't love right. But the antidote
is part of the illness, finger on a syringe gone septic, scent
like garlic burned with sage, color of nightshade.

III

Last, I have a baby not mine, a boy. He has sand all over,
even his groin. I take him into the shower, hold him under
the water. We are surrounded by men I pretend not to see.
The baby talks to me like a grown-up. They all eavesdrop.
Look, he says, pointing. *What is that?* Some seedlings start
to sprout: a garden of flora, multicolored reeds, algae rippling
the sea, behind and about his public privates. What I muffle
wants to be a scream. *Did anyone touch you?* Fear scorches
hotter than scalding water. *No,* I will him to say. *No. No. No.*
But nobody hears his answer. Not even me. Especially not me.

Et Tu

You might well ask, *Why bovine?*
Why a swan? You are Zeus. You can
take what you want. But where's the fun
in that? I like surprise. Love the hunt. Widening
eyes, resistant thighs. Fear is my ginseng, the rhino's
tusk. Some like it smooth. I like it rough.

Take Europa. She wove garlands for my neck, stroked
the grooves behind my ears, mounted my back, rode me
around the town. I could feel her flesh envelope my sinews
as I moved, a velvet blanket. It felt like love. Almost. Enough.

If there's one thing I can't stand, it is having but not keeping
the upper hand. Women who want some dumb beast they can yoke—
good luck. Easily deceived, they long, secretly—not for me—but to be
thrown down   ground into dust   legs open   mouth shut.

Year of the Rat

What I brought home from New Orleans
released no canaries flitting through maples
latticing a gravel road, visions of some
childhood good—but was prefaced by what I saw
beside the broke-down shutters
(scents of puke and gardenia)
in a pile of ice melting on Bourbon St.
after last call—a rat, cold dead,
having been, it seems,
ensconced in an ice machine
privy to pina coladas and margaritas
until fur froze, blood turned to slush,
bead-eyes shut, and ice got dumped.
I reviewed the bars I'd wandered in
over the quarter with girls' night friends.
Hoped that walking into that one bar
had not been in my Tarot cards.

But Rat has followed me across bayous and swamps,
and over time, slunk into this dream:
I search for something behind my closet door.
My room is a nightmare, of course: feather
boas, Xmas lights, boots on the loose.
Now this: A rat in a crate, not quite contained.
His nose-beak penetrates the bars,
needle teeth sink into my arm
(hotwetpanicpain)
and I am afraid to pull away, shred flesh,
gush blood. I swallow red. Screams suffocate,
choke my throat, a chasm black, thick as clay.
I am gargling God's name.

Once awake, I cannot sleep
or shake the notion
of rat-faced retribution
caught, caged, released—
its surreptitious scurry
across my sullied room
from closet to casket.

This Night

After Lee Young Lee's "At this Hour"

Tonight, my lover is playing guitar.
His tangle of cords and pedals spider the room;
his amp points away from the house and toward
the trailer park. His fingers tease the tune and build
a web of notes that ignite. Everyone can hear him,
even the horses. But what does he see when he closes
his eyes? Where is this place he goes alone? His love for me
is like a bill he forgets to pay, a reminder on the refrigerator,
left so long he no longer sees. This night, what is silent
is screaming and what is screaming goes unheard.
Tell him to turn down the volume, open his eyes.

My daughter wears earbuds, watches YouTube, seeks Anime,
reads Manga. Why is the piano buried in roses and rotten food?
Why are the girls' mouths sewn shut with X's, and why do the O's
of their eyes drip blood? Her love for me is like those stitches,
razor marks that carve my heart. Tell her to stop hurting us.
This night, what is pain is pleasure, and what is bleeding is singing.

My mother, wherever, bustles about God's kitchen, bears plates
of potatoes, beans, roast beef to lethargic angels who sit and wait.
She sits, gets up to grab the salt for Gabriel at the head of the table.
Why does she work so hard? Is happiness buried in the belly of family?
My love for her is like a feast I consume out of pleasure, not hunger.
This night, what is hungry is searching, and what is offered is empty.
Somebody tell them to open eyes and doors, come to the table, bring
their best sheep. Leave blood on the doorpost. Give, take, eat.

Found Out

For Darla

Nothing to do in Odessa, you say
but fight, fuck, and chuck rocks.
I see you back then at fifteen
all grown up, small town girl
not big on chucking rocks,
mind a wide sky, body a cherry bomb—
you, riding shotgun, eyes shut, desert hot,
shots of tequila behind the Baptist church
high noon, shotgun wedding
gunning for you.

I see you and I call you
from my same yet different state—
another girl, also home-grown,
but stagnant green terrain
spatters my little town,
a dry storm teases rain:
white lightning, white lace, white lies,
what a nothing color, white.

Escape, that swamp witch, plays
hide and seek. Shifting shapes, we seep
under the creaking screen door, insidious
as a frozen leak. Unreformed, we storm
deserts, ford torrents, frolic graves,
find and befriend unholy ghosts,
fly a wide sky once, twice, many times—
beyond unknowing, bereft of names,
those wombs we call home come morning,
skins now shed like serpents molting
molten as the stars exploding
over Odessa, Baton Rouge,
Paris, places we traverse,
shimmering the hot night
glittering god's eyes
swallowing fog at dawn.

And if we land hard, howl to find
doors painted blue windows nailed shut,
skins stuck full of rocks (such sad sacks)
locked out, laughed at, found out—
then what?
That's why we fly. There's no place like night.

Open for Business

In Back of the Attic

The topsy turvy doll lacks legs,
but that's not all. She's missing
what your mom would call
a twat. She's got
head, arms, skirt,
and underneath, a face
almost duplicate the first
but eyes brown not blue—
stare bold, head bald.

Who thought this would be fun?
Two baby girls rolled into one.
Legless, sexless, gussied up.
Wonder, have these sisters met?
Can they play? Do they whisper
in the night, conjecture what
it might be like to run, to fuck,
make babies, squirt them out?
(That's the stuff girls talk about.)

Flip Turvy over and old dust floats.
A shaft of light, if you open the curtain,
illuminates the ancient girl-child's head—
eyes faded, heart-shaped features obsolete.
The other one waits to be toppled into light,
escape that velvet tent, the dark, the heat—
where if she could, she couldn't breathe.

Stunted, broken, incomplete—but in repose,
how deep the sweet sleep
when all eyes close.

Owen County

They drank nectar
from honeysuckle and clover
August days when nothing
happened ever.

A nip and a suck
was what it took
to taste the moment
sudden sweet.

It made her livid
their mother. She'd holler,
You kids get outa them weeds
before I skin you alive.

You wanna drop dead?
They mighta been sprayed
with poison. Go on.
Just get.

She pealed potatoes
with a butcher knife
wiped it on her dress
blinked back sweat.

They weighed the odds,
ate one last flower
made sure she saw,
then scattered—

like so much
dandelion fluff—
into the buzzing afternoon.

Kemah Boardwalk in Winter

Her dad said it was too cold to ride,
though I thought he should try
to make up for all those times
Lauren rode alone.
I, too, bow out. She's not mine. Besides,
I've got kids and sins enough for one life.

The rides aren't running today, we say.
Wrong. Adolescent, defiant, she gets on
that wooden leviathan coiled for a strike.
A scornful wind bites the boardwalk,
and while we huddle, nonchalant,
Lauren rides alone.

The tracks first creak like old, slow bones,
Then the sudden clatter and clamor
takes us by surprise. We gasp: How fast
she flies! Here, then gone, again, again—
Lauren's red-mittened, uplifted hands
implore the blessing of an opaque sky.

Speechless, ashamed, we find ourselves shaken.
The breath we hold is gray. Our clasped hands tighten
as if to grasp her, this girl on the cusp of thirteen.
What fragile tethers, our numb finger, an empty net
in vain entwined. Silence crashes about these tracks.

And we would pray—if we could pray—
or words be heard over wind and surf—
out-shout the roar of train and warn
Lauren, alone, *Hold on.*

Overpowered

I caught a bumblebee in a hollyhock.
All the girls did. Kids. We didn't know
better. Incensed, he thrashed about.

Plagued, I wanted to let go. Afraid,
I clenched tighter, sweat-fingered
that pink prison.

Choked on sweet   smothered in scent
crushed by velvet—
until, irascible, he gnawed out. Buzzed off.

I won't do that again, I said, but I did—
over and over.

Working the Grave

That one winter Jen worked the grave
at Jerry's diner, but she was better
than that; she had to get out of this place—
think heavy metal on eight track tape.

The uniform boasted brown polyester—
unflattering, though someone had told her
she had a great ass. Did they mean great
as in Great Lakes? She had to wonder.

She liked to say,
If chicken fried steak is the only thing
that makes you happy working the grave,
then it's a no-brainer. You got to have it.

That, and gravy. Or the breakfast buffet—
all you can eat and don't really want.

Nights outside, the sky spit sleet. Black snow froze
under chassis. Cops swooped in when bars closed,
along with the Blacks, the Gays, and the Rednecks
(known to the Blacks and Gays as the Shit-Kickers).

There was coffee and shit-kicking going down at 3:00 A.M.
Jen wanted to bang the fry cook, but the cold silver cross
nestled in her neck's hollow told her, No. Ice cream and hot
fudge on waffles killed it when she craved a little something

sweet to get through the wait before daybreak.

Almost Eighteen:

On a blanket by the lake
five girls lean back, rest
chins against hands, heads
tilted toward a thin sun.

The scene's awash
in blues and greens,
leaves gold, the shade
that does not stay—

They know the poem
barely, recognize Monet's
watercolors in water's color.
The one in the short red skirt

and hiked-up shirt reclines,
flaunts wan skin the color
of winter. Could be she
shivers. Too cold to tan.

But the light!

It has that certain slant
exalted by the spinster
poet they want most
to forget. School's out?

Not quite. It is spring, yet—

Agamemnon at Khon's

The rooftop of Khon's Wine Bar is a great venue for tragedy, so bring lawn chairs
Modern Literature is devoted in great measure

On a muggy night in Houston, forego wine, imagine stars, and turn on the fan
to a courageous open-eyed observation of the sickeningly broken

Let it blow across the city the cold of Clytemnestra's vengeance
figurations that abound before us, around us and within

Scent of battle-sweat and entrails spliced to slit of throat, scream-engorged
And there is no make-believe about heaven, future bliss and compensation

The college-kid chorus, in Target t-shirts, remonstrates in urgent murmurs
to alleviate the utter darkness, the void of unfulfillment,

Clytemnestra slays her husband, rightfully so, along with his lover, who cannot lie
to receive and eat back the lives that have been

And you, your eyes, my murdered daughter, accuse me of nothing I did
tossed forth from the womb only to fail

And curse the nothing I do
In comparison with this, our little stories of achievement seem pitiful

(Italicized lines are from Joseph Campbell's *Hero With a Thousand Faces*)

Do the Math

I
It looks like a silk purse
if you hold it tucked under
fake kid gloves found in a bin
at the outlet center.

II
The investor says
I can tell what she will do
by what she's done in the past.
This does not bode well
for a fat-harvest future.

III
At age five, she tried
to make a pound cake
but couldn't read fractions.
This disaster was more or less
better than her later ventures.

IV
There's a row at the thrift store.
Ladies shout each other into a corner
over a throw, vintage 1975. In a line
she can't exit, she's been waiting forever—
a penny saved.

V
To affirm an underrated value
to a new generation of girls,
they made a Barbie that said
Math is fun!
but nobody bought it.

Mentors, Majors, Minors

for Kumari

When I heard about the late Jerry Bentley,
professor of history, how famous he became,
I thought about you, your great esteem
for him translated into wanting to unbutton
his top button, only, unsettle his pocket protector.
Braininess was an aphrodisiac for undergrad girls
like us: the poetry groupie, the history minor.

Tell a smart girl she's pretty, a pretty girl she's smart—
that's one way to get laid, two, if you count. We were
both pretty smart always, you better on both counts,
speed reading the diaries of Anaïs Nin, learning early
porn sells better than poetry. Or of de Beauvoir, lovely,
brainy, pages betraying she let Sartre treat her like shit.
(One is not born a woman, but rather becomes one.)
Simone had a great ass, at least in that photograph—

Well, we squandered ourselves, sleeping with artists,
disregarding a market value we never knew we had—
thinking, thinking, thinking that we mattered, our bodies
would hold, our minds be mined for unfoolish gold.
Fooled by books we read, fake claims we'd get
greatness by osmosis—
unlike Jerry Bentley, renowned historian,
the button never undone,
whose offices we frequented.

American Prairie

"I can't keep track of each fallen robin"—Leonard Cohen

Jack Kerouac spent his last few bucks on beers
to seduce two girls whose names he didn't know:
a fat brunette and his favorite, the *sullen blonde.*

Both didn't want to walk back home alone over that vast
and quiet American prairie, known for its sudden storms
and lush crops of sullen blondes. (I know. I am one).

At least Andrew Wyeth gave his girl a name,
not just space on a page. Christina owned that world,
he said, so she did. If you name it, you own it—

Jack never owned jack, much less some bird.
You don't own me later sang a new slough of tough girls
in stretch pants and bouffants, girls with names you forget

or never knew. Not the way you knew Nancy, whose white
boots never walked a mile in *this* sullen blonde's shoes
traipsing, down-in-the-heel, over that flat expanse of field

no one seemed to own, quivering like a sheath of wheat,
never gathered, cast off as chaff, with neither oak for shade,
nor boulder to hide behind—a mere mirage of fluid light

or blurr on a boxcar swallowed by
the ruthless, indifferent,
merciless sky.

Once Upon Eden

we are just kids
        that moment when
we turn the glass over
        and touch
time caught in a net
        melts like a snow cone
seeps to the edge
        spills cherry on the lawn
hands hair breath
        wheels spun webs woven
cut paper wrap rock
        on hot concrete
bloom balloons plumb purple
        bang
fervent dirges verdant worlds
        beat
heart-shaped death bells
        pop
like that condom
`   each and every
garden of broken

Witness

That faded high-top sneaker hanging
from my barbed-wire fence
bears witness:

Teen lovers tipping cows, laughing,
downing Strawberry Hill on ice
one July-hot night. A dry storm drives

across the sky. New grass and goldenrod
cling to their jeans, and they forget about
curfew, forget everything:

the long trek back to the road, those lies
to devise, her shoe stuck in the wire,
their headlong pitch, how his hunger

traced her abraded thigh, her taste—
iron and salt and wet.

Two months later, huddled in a bathroom,
they stare at a tube, wait for hues to unbleed:
blue for go and pink for forget-about-it.

Do they hold hands? So much has been
lost by then, it doesn't matter.
They barely remember—

We all sported red Keds,
swigged soda pop wine
one sweet summer.

Wedding Ring Quilt

Dragonfly
Sampan
Wisteria
Palm

How many lunes
splinter suns
make moons
become
this womb encompassing

oceans
raindrops
wide sighs
small yawns
ecstasy

and this
the kiss
that dances distraught
delves intense
alights air

whispers
like leaves
like lust
like love
like dust

Greasy Spoon

Why He Never Married

He'd miss every train in the station
scarfing Bellinis, a drink he didn't like,
in the closest bar, with a babe named Blair
or Brook or was it Brett? No, that's the girl in a book
by F. Scott, or Hemingway, maybe? One with bullfights,
a man, a secret, some temptress, Tempranillo, cigars—
anyway, that was the look he was going for.

These days when he takes a plane, he makes sure
to notice where the exits are. A stewardess waves his gaze
one way or another. She looks fine in gabardine, wears wings
like beacons. Lufthansa boasts a full bar, but Air Singapore—
those girls are to die for. What an expression! Was there ever
a woman to live for? He orders a Singapore Sling, zones out
on the *Dreamy Clouds, Gossamer Sky*—names of the paint
his ex had wanted to buy, wonders why he isn't on the aisle,
and who names paint?

Sometimes at night his restless leg kicks in. His lover's hand
on his agitated thigh reminds him he can't sleep and leave
at the same time

Calling It Wrong

When he took me to *Madame Butterfly,* I knew
I should of wore black.
These women got good gams, Italian shoes,
shoulders like Samurai swords—and here I am
made in Walmart. *Don't dress up,* he said.
He don't know what that means to me.

First time I heard *Madame Butterfly*
I was watching Glynn Close, pregnant, beyond glum,
blubbering in the dark, stood up by Michael Douglas
home fondling his pretty wife. So boil the family bunny
find the nearest knife—Poor Glynn!
Anyway, she died.

It went better for Julia Roberts. sitting snazzy
in that private jet, pocket candy for Richard Gere.
Lucky Julia! She got the guy—
proving red heads *can* wear red,
prostitutes *do* love opera,
and pretty women cry quite nicely
over all the right parts.

I cry too. Madame Butterfly
wanes, moonfaced, as the moon
makes its way to the lake.
Music blooms. Come morning
slick with crumpled blossoms,
tear cracks in her mask,
she waits, blindfolds the baby,
makes sure *he* sees.

Nothing wrong with this life falling on a sword won't fix.

Poor Butterfly. Somebody should of told her,
Honey, don't bother wearing black.
This ain't no late night movie.
Think Glynn, not Julia.
A butterfly is a butterfly is a butterfly—
symbolism not lost, even on me.

The Blood Never Lies

After D.H. Lawrence

But it does
rationalize

the hand's breadth
between us

is good
as a smile

the near miss
when we kiss

accidental

all shells
are fragile

in sleep
if you flinch

when we touch
it means nothing

much

Because Primavera Is Not a Pasta

for Sandro Botticelli's Primavera

Remember that time I barfed up breakfast
because I was pregnant and abandoned in Italy
and then went to the Uffizi to see the Botticelli's?
No? Didn't think so. You had to be there. No-show.
Too bad you broke up with me at the airport.
Bad for me at least. Sent packing, so to speak.
Way before *Eat, Pray, Love* was thought of.
Quite the opposite of that chick flick, the day
I learned that Primavera is not a pasta.

But wait! Let me share.

First, green everywhere. Me, queasy.
The man on the left, knight-errant, leans
limp against a spindly tree, stares up
like, *Look, it's the Goodyear blimp.*
Three nymphs do a Maypole dance
for his viewing pleasure. They seem
a bit pregnant. He might be the father.

The man on the right, gray-shaded demon,
grabs a stray pagan, got a bun in her oven.
Her friend has been hiding the sausage again.
In this grove of quickening women and evasive
men, I count six girls, all about six months gone.

But wait! That's me in the middle, flora-adorned.
Got my rose garlands on, but I'm doe-eyed, alone,
forlorn in Florence, other-worldly in the Uffizi,
fertile in myrtle like the Centaur next door—
not to mention
swoll-ankled, faun-stuck, itchy-crotched, knocked up.

O fantasy! Stump-dumb as a deer, still I'm tragically
aware: this will be my first and last visit here
in Botticelli's Italy.

Pop Quiz at the Clinic

Have you had more than ten sexual partners?
Hasn't everyone?
Just Yes or No, please.
Yes.

Have you ever had sex with a gay or bisexual partner?
Successfully?
Yes or No, please.
No.

Have you ever used IV drugs?
I don't like needles.
Yes or No.
Yes.

When was the last time you had sexual intercourse?
I don't remember.
That long ago?
That unmemorable.

Do you use protection?
My heart is a prophylactic.
Is that a yes or a no?
Yes.

You're going to feel some pressure.
I already do.
Does that feel cold?
Yes.

Does this hurt?
Yes.
Any itching? Burning? Bumps?
no. No. NO.

Last One: Do you believe in the clandestine dance of transcendent souls?
You need me to answer Yes or No?
Yes.
No.

Silver Mine

Let's go to New Mexico. I'll pay for everything, you said.
On the road we road we read *Dharma Bums*
crooned Townes all the way to El Paso
browsed the Van Gogh bookstore in Van Horne
(another Sunflower Sutra)
got high in Valentine
Marfa lights dark
museum closed on Sunday.

But the cottonwoods were gold
as desert dust, Spanish doubloons
glinted like the eyes of Cortez
and fractured light flitted fuchsia
love-beads at that Madrid hippie hotel.
Dream catchers and kachina dolls—
What didn't we buy in Santa Fe?

Snapshots: Thanksgiving in Los Cerillos—
chili on everything, red or green?
Silver mines defunct, turquoise
stripped by Anasazi—
who knows how
long gone?

Now you mail me letters scribbled on a bus,
vintage 1948, your writer's garret
that doesn't run
but sports a view
cluttered with junk:
home-made Henry Miller crosses,
sculpted from dead TV's stacked up.

You grow blue corn, drink alone
so frail now my outlaw lover
listening to Guy Clark cassettes
(Desperados Waiting for a Train)
too dissipated to disappear
in Mexico like Ambrose Bierce
looking for a revolution—
any war will do.

And you were wrong. We both paid.
I read your letters, write sometimes.

A Love Story, of Sorts

You arrived at my door
in shorts, expiration date
tattooed to your left thigh
blurred by hangover not quite
obscured by lack of sleep.

I spent a lot of time
telling you goodbye,
wired to anticipate
the rotten demise,
the short shelf life.

Might be you'd cheat
or I'd get bitter
not so bored by you
as by myself with you—
sacrament of the self-effaced.

Or one of us might die,
perhaps even of natural causes.
Are we common-law,
or just common?
About my will—It's been misplaced.

In any case, it seems
you have outlived
my low expectations,
maybe received a reprieve?
Could be. But still—

Not one to be caught off guard,
I kill us off out of habit.

Sweet Warm Strong

This morning under a milky sun
I drank the espresso and honey
you left me
watched wild things saunter or soar out of the woods
behind my house—an ambling possum, squabbling jay,
and my favorite, the feral Tom. If I feed him
he leaves me
a bird, a mouse, himself—
Will he ever call me *home*?

Today an urgent appointment with freedom
beckons you both. I want to warm my coffee
but I might miss how the warblers flirt and flit
singing what they want
along the fence line,
past the hammock
where you held
my hand that time—

It is a cold good
the sweet sip I cup
in my not-so-open palm
as long as you let me.

Kenning

"A hole is to Dig"—Maurice Sendak

He is digging a hole
for her to plant a peach tree.
She says peaches are good feng shui,
and they need the shade, though it rained today.

She is out and about listening to poetry
or drinking martinis at the Rainbow Lodge
with friends. *Music on 19th Street,* she texts him.
He texts back, *Still digging.*

She thinks he thinks it's the least he can do
like unpacking the basket that holds his clothes
so he can go off alone on short notice. It's domestic stuff
that makes you stuck.

This isn't the first hole he has dug, but this one feels good.
The ground is hard and it's a simple goal to make her smile
after all she covers over—trifles, treasures, bones—
holes she dug on her own.

She comes home a little drunk
(she drinks too much) seems pleased
with her peach tree, sallow sentry in the scant
Houston breeze. She babbles on about some poem

she heard extolling the virtues of sea turtles,
their long crawl out of ocean, no bunny-hop of faith,
then digging in dark, only to fill a hole with delicate eggs—
until the inevitable retreat at dawn

inching back to the whale road, reptile brains nescient,
never knowing which will breathe, live, thrive—
too simple to hope some make it
after all.

Seahorses Sleep Intertwined

But do soul mates mate for life?
Like, say, gibbons, or the Marconi penguins?

After lifetimes together, do soul mates still
howl like gray wolves, yowl like barn owls?

Soar in tandem as bald eagles do?
Can they get it on like shingleback skinks?

Are they randy as beavers?
Do they go black vulture on each other?

I mean, at least once a week (or maybe two)
Or do they, like humans—say, like me and you—

wonder in bed, is my account overdrawn?
Was that leftover meatloaf way too old?

And if we shop online, just where can we find
some discreet Kama Sutra for the animal soul?

Grazing

It's not a meal if nothing dies:
the deer, pausing by a pond; the steer,
balls tossed in a bucket, long ago gone.

Dead flesh is made succulent
by marinating, braising, pounding—
broken down to please the palate

all resistance gone.
What I do to meat,
you do to me.

Melon vines sprawl across
two rows of pungent mulch—
oddly fragrant.

Yellow flowers transform overnight.
We always miss the moment
bloom becomes food.

We used to watch and wait but always
I turn my gaze away
and everything has changed.

Stale Mate

You are not allowed to put yourself in check,
so you keep yourself in check.
He is bored with this game.

He elaborates on his theory that dreams
are mathematical. You watch him draw lines:
This is time. There's space. Here is your room.

But you don't stay.

The dream room you invade is ensconced in glass.
Inside, you hold a cloisonné chalice of wine. Outside,
rain. Headlights glint silver, gleam panes.

This wedding reception is yours, the one they threw
when you were gone. So, go on: toast your own
exquisite bliss. In life, no champagne, just this

checkered board where only two moves are open
and you make them again and again, as if
one could possibly win.

Before the Storm

We thought it was because we gave up
that we stayed in this place where nothing
changes but lightbulbs, the cat box, and daylight
savings time. Our pockets emptied and filled like tides,
clouds, beach balls, sex, accordions, New Orleans—
the sax that breathes a blue note
as long as the lungs hold out.

When the rains came, what a racket! Banging
keys to the kingdom against a Salvation Army can,
saying, *Get in line.* Like kids, we cry:

Mama can we play in the rain? Strip down to our skivvies,
grab a bar of Palmolive? Moses ain't made it off that mountain.
yet. We got time. Need me something shiny and gold to roll
around my mouth. Goddamn manna, Mama, good for nobody
but beggars and squatters. Gimme some of them grapes,
the kind they got in Canaan, juicy like I like.

We'll only get struck by lightning if we're lucky.

Baby, I'm Yours

Everybody's somebody's Daisy. Did Gatsby
in his cool blue pool reflect for a moment
before bleeding the chlorine a shade like maple
leaves after summer?

Love, love, oh careless love—

Ask old Somerset Maugham; every woman's one man's
Mildred, the classic class-less anemic waitress.
How she slashes his curtains, gouges his eyes
with her itty-bitty nail file while he holds her hand:

such a little prick—
open wide.

Yes, sir, that's my baby

For there's a Faustus in all of us: We'd rather
fuck Helen of Troy than drink the blood of Christ.
Every woman wants to be Helen;
every Adam meets his Eve,

the one
to take a drag on his death stick,
the one to finish him off.

Pyre

It had to go, that hedge. It hid the bones
of the house. Unruly greenery. The day
their daughter left for college, they strafed
the place, pyre of compost on the lawn.
Girl tore off in her cherry Mustang, didn't cry.

Wife thought a face lift would work, help sell
the house. Oops paint, cheap, Burnt Ochre,
looked more like Burnt Okra. She didn't count
on all that was broken. The mirror, she broke it.
The phone, he broke it. The kids, maybe therapy
would fix them. She was fixing to fix them,
as they say in Texas, but she too, was broke.

And that strata, closets of rubble, what to do
but paw through, discard, decide. Easter picture,
bunny-eared family? Wife frazzled, husband bored.
Pitch it. Chinese nesting tables, useless—his.
Mission bed, heavy, unwieldy—hers. Garage sale
goods for Purple Heart. Furniture not fit for the condo
she'd picked; at odds in Hell, where he was headed,
she knew for sure.

Unable to sell, Ex-Wife (now) rented the house
to a Russian woman who sold furs for Sakowitz
and stuffed that den with armoires, carved tables,
stacking dolls, bronze panthers, all that loot smuggled
from St. Petersburg before the fall. And Persian rugs,
let's not forget, plopped on terra cotta tiles, hiding flaws
innate to Saltillo—mistakes, footprints baked in apricot
clay one warm day on some faraway mesa. What kind
of critter? Domestic or wild? Kitty or coyote? Who knows?

Tiles bought for those footprints, remnants of what was once
nameless and alive.

Crossing the Trinity River

I came on the field where we saw the snow geese
last winter, white on white, myriads, who knows
their number, why they stopped on their way
to where, or how briefly they would stay.

Today I replayed that day —how we trudged snow
to get my red dress, velvet as a Valentine's dance.
That hot hot shower in a house of ice, furnace clunking.
Then later, quilt-covered, singing *We'll go honkey tonkin'*—

We drove backroads, hard-froze, to waltz a drafty dance hall,
though as I recall, on that occasion—all winter, even—
we were never cold.

This morning, the field is gold-filled with flowers, bright like
lemon drops. The sun is a peach that fell from your tree,
and all the world hums April-warm and sweet
except for you and me.

Post-Church Lunch

The Stuff They Feed Us

You are what you eat
said Enkidu to his hooker friend

A moment on the lips
said Persephone to her pomegranate

Knowledge is power
said Eve nakedly petulant

Power corrupts
God huffed

Absolutely
Satan smiled

Fragrant, fruity, not without a bite
Socrates swirled the wine

Thank you, no, not another bite
Buddha drooled on the rice

I never found the food I liked
a hungry Kafka hissed

Don't wanna be big and strong
the angry child sniffed

Wonder Bread, Kool-Aid
the body, the blood of Christ—

Open wide.

The Fault in your Stars

for my father

Your telescope in our backyard
ran rings around Saturn, ogled Mars.
I had to stand on a block to look, lens wet
as the breath of country Kentucky night.

Years later we perused maps of the stars,
constellations, the Southern cross, Thai skies
littered with light. You said stars don't really
know our destiny. God knows. I believed.

And in between, we landed on the moon
stayed up late, drank Tang. Skeptics said
it was all fake. How'd the flag move, sans wind,
even oxygen? I began to question your position.

At ten, that leap from concrete to abstract,
led me to attack answers you would never retract.
Why did you act so knowing, so smug?
When Atlas dropped the world, it landed with a thud.

Of all the things you told me, only your telescope
stayed in place, squarely, traced heaven's trajectory—
the Big Bang, which you claimed, was only a theory.
Or so you told me, wobbly on tiptoe, straining to see.

Evangelizing Zion Hill:

Kentucky, 1972

Take the road over Elkhorn Creek at Weisenberger Mill.
Ford Falcon ragtop, 1965. Red stripe, round tail lights.
Top down. Noon heat. Cracked vinyl, thigh-stuck seats.
I know this road, its every bend. Me, girl in the backseat,
twelve years tired. Buzz of broken radio. Eyes shut to blot
how light lands on asphalt. Hard. White-fenced pastures.
Occasional dappled shadows.

My father teaches my brother to drive a stick shift. Ease up
on the clutch. Don't lurch. Slow down around the bend.
Avoid surprise. Try not to die. But wait! A whirring rush
of sun-splashed water. The mill! Then, the clamor:
Let's get out! Watch it work! How do they make cornmeal?
How, flour? Those paddles smack of magic. My father sifts
his ready-made answer: Separate chaff from wheat. Water churns.
Wheel turns. Inside grinds. It's not hard. Remember why we're here.

We don't get out.

Now stop. Knock on the first door: shotgun house, red geraniums.
The preacher: fat, Black, poor, like everyone in Zion. Asks us in,
bent on discussion. Doesn't happen often. A holy roller, for sure.
My father proffers a Watchtower. Wields a Bible. Refers to scripture:
Last days. Good news. Kingdom of heaven. But the preacher,
in a sweat of fervor, waves hammy hands. Nay-says "doctrine."

He insists, "You can't fathom the Bible if you don't get happy."
Asks us, "Don't you ever get happy?" Dad shakes his head,
dodges the question. Beware of demons. Satan is mistaken
for an angel of light. Me, I'd gladly hear the preacher speak
in tongues of angels. Get ecstatic. Or utter gibberish, gutteral
phonemes—hack, lisp, squawk, sing. Spit split pea soup—
like Linda Blair in that movie I'd heard of but never seen—
Say something, anything I couldn't, wouldn't
understand: fruit flung far from the tree
past my grasp, jettisoned beyond
my father's ready hand.

But we leave.

Preacher, still eager to instruct us, sees us to the door.
Watches how fast we walk our walk, lest he talk his talk.
Sees us shake the dust off our feet. I could've told the man,
Ease up. We don't believe in getting happy. Not us.

So Much for Orgies in the Temple

She wanted to be a bride when she grew up
perhaps a priestess, an oracle, or a virgin sacrifice—
she couldn't decide.

When her soul disowned her body,
shoved it off satiate like a lover
collapsed across her chest—
what a mess—
her body collected itself with the dignity
of a condom wrapper tossed in the corner,
showered and accessorized
from the five and dime,
polished her pumps, painted
her mouth Crimson Abandon,
then, slick as sin,
said *There must be a party somewhere,*
as if on a mission.

When her body sloughed off her soul—
consigned it to the rag bag
like last fall's gabardine pants—
her soul, thus renounced,
uncrumpled and flounced
off righteous as a bride
to file for a pricey divorce,
then took to her chamber
unencumbered
by pesky demands of the flesh—
free to paint teacups, read the epistles
of St. Paul, listen to sonatas, write sonnets
like John Donne, without bringing anyone
a beer, while she was up.

What I Took

What I took to be safety
was a folding chair stuck to my thighs.

What I thought was the long arm of God
turned out to be a gray man sweating a gabardine suit.

What I took to be love
was a dirty hanky folded to hide what was nasty.

What I thought was a woman with a blonde beehive,
well, she was heartlessness.

What I took to be sin,
a ticket on the longest subway with only a hint of light.

What I thought was the smell of dogshit in my Honda Civic
turned out to be obedience.

(I knew because nobody said nothing).

What I took to be truth,
some scribble scrabble that someone said was a tree.

What I thought was a spider squatting in the corner,
now,that was a submissive woman.

What I took to be sex
was a mountain with a portal and a magic word I couldn't guess

hard as I tried.

What I took to be creation
turned into a page of begets and a map crumpled with fault lines.

What I took to be God, always
some red-crayon madness I could never paint over on account of the
grease.

Bible Banger

Meetings three times a week
I remember the temperature:
skin stuck to hard back chairs
come summer, then in winter
soles melting over a radiator.
Good God.

In the graveyard
we played at persecution
assured of what would happen:
paraded naked down the street,
trussed up, forced to fornicate,
abstinence a crazy game
for righteousness' sake.

It was the best of times
the End of Tmes.

I'm still angry with your angry God
spewing poison on my clean white psyche,
a fetish born every turn, open season on
all them whores of Babylon.
Unforgiveness happens

Drunks
adulterers
perverts
addicts
homosexuals
dissenters
you
will
burn
in Hell

So say the signs wielded by
bow-tied folks outside the zoo.
Pretty children on the train
don't know how
they got loose.

Shotgun, Third Ward #1
After the painting by John T. Biggers, 1966

The church, a burnt
offering to the gods
of hate; the children
dancing on the ashes,
their mothers, grave.

Entrails of smoke
float. The bell melts.

Been a while
since Satan slept.
One less scripture
to forget: *Blessed are*
and *Jesus wept*.

Green Yin

So in my dream it was dark
and I was at your Father's table
only not; I was hiding just behind
the door, and folks were talking
about church, and I said I'd rather
clear a forest of pine and deciduous
trees than go to church and your father
got mad and roared like the old Jehovah
in that scary book.

Wait. I'm not finished.

Then your mother, who's dead,
took me to the kitchen (the place
of alchemy) And there was this green
rug on the floor, bright, bright, bright
and wet to my bare feet. It felt
like moss, but wetter. Algae.
I have a rug just like this,
I told her.

I know you do, she said.

Then you dreamed of my kitchen
(the place of alchemy) and it was bright,
bright, bright, and there was this cactus
looking kind of phallic, but blooming red.
It's pretty, you said. Too bad about
the thorns. And your mother,
who's dead, said,
What it needs is light.

What Moses Didn't Know

It wasn't the fleshpots
of Egypt we missed
but the family recipe.
We are famished.

This manna, this tepid
white God-stuff you gave us
we didn't work for
and we don't want.

It kills appetite, not hunger.
We hunger for kill
for something to tear
with our teeth.

It wasn't the golden calf
we worshipped,
or frenzy of flesh we wanted
but meat.

Jagged Light

Sun dapples your back. You sit on the edge
of my bed, unpropelled to stay or leave.
If I say *Stay*, you fidget—restless—hedge.
I'm not the muse I used to be. This grief
slices sharp—a shaft of light, but jagged—
unfurls wrinkles, scars, bruises, broken veins.
Night-pretty, come morning, pretty ragged,
I don a robe, ungainly fears contained.
I want to leave my body in the dust.
Our truth of being, the enlightened say,
is not this flagging mass of hungers—lusts—
It's incandescence trapped in urns of clay.
But fasting, praying never gave me Grace—
This battered vessel's portal to that place.

By the Sword

When I see couples fight
over the shower curtain
her drinking, his mother,
his-and-her
robes crumpled
abandoned
in separate rooms—
I feel smug,
amused,
sad.

I, too, ate rage
for breakfast, smoked
my man like that first
cigarette of the day,
drove to the rifle range
for target practice,
weathered battles,
planned espionage,
dug foxholes,
sniped.

But today, this soldier's
sword is plunged hilt-deep
in dirt. I got crops to plant,
fields to plow, seeds
to redeem. Morning's
too sweet to waste.
Look! The sun is high
the season, late.

Incantation

When New Age was new, we tried to bend spoons
made mojos of spit and sweat, burned lovers' hair
chanted *Om Nama Shivaya* and the Jesus prayer.
We knew we could master mind over matter
make men adore us, bid fortune come for us.
We were twenty, not fifty, with no long litany
of mishaps, disasters, nasty divorces,
buyer's remorses, and
blown-off-courses.
.

Headed for that second surgery
she said *Don't send me positivity.*
Keep your healing vibes. Pray if it makes
you feel better. For me, it's the opium of bitter,
broken in half, sunk in water, downed with wine.
She ran a race that week, concrete under her feet,
mind over matter. I named it *Cancer*. What does it matter
it's only a road? I pray like a poet that she runs like a warrior
over that finishing line.

Prayer to the God of Small Good

Oh, God of small good, whose lair is under the dishwasher,
when I asked for luck, pristine plates, that no gadgets break
during my upcoming dinner-with-friends—

Behold! You sent me a rat.

True, I was born in the year of the rat, a fact auspicious
in summer but not in winter, according to folklore. Hoarders
like me, you see—Rats—find pickings slim in a snowstorm

of the blue norther sort that formed when I was born. Forced
to harvest baubles, Christmas tinsel, inedibles, I am—have been—
famished for eons, a Dickensian orphan. But it seems you mistook

what I asked. Or perhaps you answer in symbols, like those other
gods I no longer harbor, having dumped that stock in their river
before the last crash. So when the rat meandered out, mid-dinner,

commenced to picking kibble from the cat bowl, looked my guests
straight in their incredulous eyes—well, we dropped our drumsticks.
I asked for luck. You sent me a rat.

It smarted like a childhood taunt:
Nanny Nanny Boo Boo. Look where your prayers get you.
Plead for peace? Feed the poor? Some dumb luck?

Watch what you want. Get over the answer. No favor is ever so small
it cannot be refused. Oh, God who grants the opposite of fortune,
send me a scorpion.

In the Know

Enough about the snake. I was empty as slate.
It wasn't me who deemed serpents phallic, fruit
symbolic. I was a dolt, ignorant, daft as a trout.
It was the tree who shook his branches at me.

I've got a secret I'm not telling he teased, sing-song,
girlie, his real voice deep as a pit. I wanted. Reached.
At that moment, a serpent toppled out, twined about
the fruit. I leaned in as he began to speak: *Believe me,*

Eve. You don't know what you don't know. Try it, he said.
I did. That was no apple I bit. Its taste lopped off the top
of my head. Knowledge streamed in thick as ambrosia,
a word I learned when taut flesh broke and nectar flowed

down my throat. I saw the Greeks, their snowy statues
and knew about Plato before he sprang from my loins.
I knew the word *loins* and named the lions. My dominion
flowed from the garden into the Euphrates, the Ganges,

the Amazon, called after strident women not carved of rib.
I learned about Sartre (to do is to be) and Simone (*one is not
born but rather one becomes a woman.*) I ran to Adam, said,
Try this, He did. Flushed red. Handed me a leaf, told me *Hide*

from the big guy. And you know the story: cast from the garden,
doomed to crave my husband, bound to hurt in childbirth. But did
this dissever the sieve of sweet ether one nibble placed in my brain?
Laughable, what got jotted down in history. The irony! Seduced?

Maybe. Naïve, yes. Entitled, definitely. I took what I wanted,
what should have been mine. This, I believe:
I am not now, nor was I ever
deceived.

Crooked Mile Café

I Dreamed a Crooked Mile

I was walking above a river,
road snaking hard, trees shading
remnants of a just-sunk sun,
that fall of fire and water
sloping steep, the dusk
darkly red.

I came to a house on the corner
of nothing, the lawn surprising green,
walls once-adjacent, now broken
as if they had drifted—
I spied the for-sale sign and
nosed in.

Narrow from without, the room
opened to wood floors, sopping,
water dripping sun-splashed walls,
light slicing the quiet wet
of all those windows—

So much empty
shushing through.

And I knew it for my own
would sell it all, my cloak, my soul
barter my only to buy it over time—
this fecund broken mansion
always   already   always
mine.

Three Poems about our Brief Encounter

I
Loneliness seeps insidious
as the fluids we tried to not trade,
makes me want you to say
stay as much as I want to
leave. It is a long way
driving
in the dark.

II
You hold a mirror up to me, claim,
Look at you, brilliant, becoming—
What's not to like?
When you drop it, carelessly
or purposely, and it shatters,
do I break?

III
I think If I were a guy,
I could get this right,
no intrigues, no need
to decorate empty rooms
with cobwebs and glitter.
I would stand in a bright river
thigh-high in waders, unswayed,
skip stones on water,
catch trout.

There would be cigars, laughter,
reflective moments, quiet, not
ethereal, real as the silver
fish in your hand, the one
you can keep or toss back
with hardly a mark,
you think.

Beggars Feast

When you ask me to stay the night
it was like God gave me candy,
plunked me on the ferris wheel
over Santa Monica Pier
sugar melting like Icarus' wings
feathers spun around the carousel
(unicorns, roosters, flighty things)
into the breathless blue.

I want to wake with the sun
splashing your face, let you
call me Sweetie, not say
you love me, only
believe.

Come Sunday, we speak in tongues
fill holy those ghosts skulking the corners
of hungry dark. We dust away spiders
shriveled on sills, smear grime off glass,
rap an urgent *Open*
(knuckles knocking panes sealed shut)
beg for blue, beseech the sun,
borrow milk from a morning moon.

All hollow, save for this
praise song.

Valentine

Look at you in your red dress
the Queen of Hearts, he says
warming the swirling wine
and next thing you're naked
under the cold
white sheet
of a Montrose clinic
your blood filling vial
after vial, this red less
the color of passion
than shame.

Something is missing
from this story
I know.

Shoo-Fly Pie

I didn't go to Harvard but I'm smart
enough to know I'm daft
as that Flannery O'Connor character,
the girl who got left behind in the diner.

And if someone had taught me to say *bird,*
I just might just fly this coop where gingham women
reel off specials like crazed Betty Crockers: *You got to try*
the chicken-fried chicken. Want some coffee with that sugar?

I'd lick the Cool Whip off my lips, not wipe them
on my shirt. I'd clear that plate of shoo-fly pie
you left behind that time you ate and didn't pay.
Even you're supposed to dig for change. That's right.

Somebody always has to pay.

Monsters

When I crossed the causeway, that black chasm
filled with fog made plain my confusion:
It is only a road, a straight shot, and whether
you are hard or kind   kind of hard   hardly kind
is not a question that is mine to answer.

So stuff grape leaves, pet the cat,
let latent snakes slither out of your brain.
I will eat them or not, wear them as a token
of your affection, bright about my neck,
heavy as lead. I am a simple sort

of vampire, like to lollygag
in my hammock, plan my feast.
I need the blood of lovers—
Good, because you bleed
profusely and on demand.

Show me your wound, I'll show you mine.
Nothing happened to warrant this.
There's a cure and we don't want it.

The Realist Tutors his Eager Scholar

"For The Gust of Wind," Oil painting by Gustave Courbet

But you talk like a Romantic.
It is a "gust" not a "thrust" of wind.
There is no intent. Nature is indifferent.
Lightning lights on the highest point, the most
accessible target in an open field. This verdant
green evokes the O of a childish ego, hoodwinked
by transcendental hoodoo, unaware that feelings
are negligible. Trees don't fight or submit to fate,
skies don't weep, nor do storms ravish innocence.
Pods fall, seeds spill against law or will. No need
wonder about the drought before or after that shout
of thunder, months of whispers, insidious, rasping,
Will it ever rain again?

Cruelty is man's domain. It requires effort, forethought,
makes us the animal-namers, nature-rulers. Still, you ask,
Why paint? If I am right, why commemorate something so
fleeting, signifying nothing? I don't concede the point. Art
stokes our illusion of control—that's the truth about beauty.
Storms happen sans intention; we claim them for reflection.
Such is the nonsense of romance. Forgive—or not—my rant:
It is an infant's sensitivity, my dear, though a most endearing
flaw, your headstrong inability to process indifference.

Goblin Mine

I grabbed you from the black back
of my witch's hat. You took my cloak,
made me disrobe, cuddled and suckled
my devil's mark. You looked small and dark—
all brain and cock—dimmed the light and got to work.
My eyes, they hurt, was your remark.

You are so fetching, so you said.
Fetch, roll over, beg, play dead.
Fetch something cold to cool my cauldron mind,
something smooth to soothe my eyes, my eyes,
never resting, reddening all the time. Will I sicken,
grow old, die, go blind? Fear buzzed you like a power line.

Yes, yes, yes, and maybe—
You can't sleep because you're crazy.
Is that the comfort that you want? It's all I got.
What about Milton? He was blind. He still could whelp
those hounds of hell, that hot hole where they come and go.
You're the monster scholar; you should know.

Fuck Milton, you said, *He's overrated. Hurry, help me*
get dream-stated. Find the place. Uncoil my psyche like a snake.
The light, the light, it hurts my eyes. Make haste and haze
my oh-so-harsh, my name resembles prison bars.

I looked, and my, you'd grown up fast—your face
had grown a god-head mask. Who knew
when I plucked you out of my hat
that I could never put you back?

Leda and the Swan: the Remix

Her friends said, Leda, don't play dumb.
You had to know you were screwing Zeus.
With cunning body, mismanaged mind,
unopened volume of Faust or Proust—
you try for a guy with a Pushcart prize,
when you fuck, like to knock his book awry.

But in that demi-compartment just outside
his unholy house of many mansions
he keeps you, makes you memorize
a litany of obsessions: disease, his eyes,
the wife he's too bored by to bed or hate,
the escargot he made and gave
to the cat who has proved his most cherished prize,
unlike humdrum humans he loves to despise.

Leda, what did you think that you'd achieve?
Thought you'd get by osmosis a Harvard degree?
Be undeceived: The foot of that ladder he's been
trying to climb is littered with writers he deems
not-quite-prime-time. He will steal your peace,
piece by piece, a placebo for sleep. And when
he drops you at last from his ruthless beak,
you will know the vastness
of relief.

Tastes like Hemlock

Like the way the venom rolls like old merlot
off my honey-tongue, summer slow? Oh no,
go south. Eels electrify my mouth, rattlers rustle
sea grass, water moccasins swarm the swimming hole,
coral snakes nibble mango toes. They're potent but slow.

Tell the truth:
Who does spite right? Who does bitter better? Want some
sugar with my cyanide? Who said you get to pick your poison?

Lover, lover, darling husband, would-be wife—no need tie
that tourniquet tight. Cassandra bitches but she don't bite.
Close your eyes, wet your whistle, open wide, hold your nose.
Toss it back like Cuervo gold.
Swallow.

Crashing

I can't recollect emotion in tranquility don't
recall the last time you touched me only see you
recumbent remember you told me I was beautiful
in my blue robe we were eating sushi after and I don't
know what to do with the disconnect I am trifled with want
to walk down dusty roads alone remember Tennessee ferns
red dirt can't think what it was I wanted to eat moon cakes
for the new year go out for eggs benedict like we used to drive
around North Shore sugar cane Hasegawa's Shave Ice Hawaiian
weddings a hundred dollars no that was someone else it all tumbled
into the rough surf when I rounded that turn at Big Sur dreaming of
Nepenthe I came to someone's empty bungalow drank their pinot noir
played their Billie Holiday 45s dozed in their sheets Egyptian cotton
like the Pharaoh planned his place in the Hamptons you have to paint
it just right or it doesn't wake up in the afterlife there is always water
sometimes sand like the beach or the desert or just grit it's hard to tell
what does that mean I will have to ask Henry he'll consult Jung I drive
my Spitfire up hills of Manoa or Wilhelmina Rise start to slide at the light
I'm not wired for second gear no idle only zero or one hundred now I'm
zero.

Going to the Fair

Oh no, not another Nordic blonde—
wide-eyed, the kind
you like to glut your sweet tooth on—
Think you'll gnaw away at this soft one?

Lovely fruit not ripe to fall
into your lap, lap you up
juices slickening lascivious chin—
She won't hobnob with goblin men.

You can't taste her wares for a paltry penny
spew your poison across her mind
carve poems dark in ivory skin
not even with your phallic pen—

You'll never stain her white clean sheets
sully the keepsakes that she keeps, sate
the black hole where your heart ought to be—
She's happy. And good, too good, too good for you—

Take it from me.

What I Didn't Say

The purest people are sluts you said
so we pried boards off of the floor
and slipped into the swamp this house
was built on, the air thick like cake
so black we had to trace a path
with lantern hands.

The way mud sucks boots off feet,
razors crave to carve your name
in my arm, penicillin needs
disease, heroin a vein,
I loved you.

First frost melts the night a shade
of bright that does not last.
Love is a fist.

And you are the face I see in the drapes
I didn't close, the saboteur that waits
in restaurants, the sweat I imagine
on window panes.

If you come to my door do not knock
I would never tell you no I will
never tell you
No.

Boarded Shut

Birthmark

If you run
your hands
through
my hair
you find
the point
at the back
of my brain
scissor-sharp
where forceps
clamped
and dragged me
into light
the smack
the scream
my mother
can't remember
on her own
psychotic episode
that eradicated pain
made her forget
nightmares ensuing
drugs
to dry her up
I was a bitch
of a baby
cried for 40 days
in her wilderness
no respite
only my skull
bears witness
like the mark
you carry
no one sees
the soft spot
shaped by that
which brought
you out
in spite

Dormer

If the roof were lifted off this house,
      like the dollhouse of your dreams,
would stratus clouds drift silent, wintry,
      waft across the indoor-outdoor carpet,
avocado green, cloak the orange curtains, ignited always
        at sunset, in time for Walter Cronkite or Walt Disney
          on Sunday?

Would clouds flow over the low rattan table
      which could have been heightened but wasn't,
its pie-wedge chairs seating kids-turned-adolescent,
      hunched over Monopoly, reluctant to adjust for fear
        and hope they'd have to leave?
          Everyone leaves.

Winter scene from dormer: ice eaves, trees (sparse in summer)
      de-leaved, spindly, branches brittle, overreaching.
        Lightning rods, really, apt to splinter, crash, catch fire,
      come the hard freeze. We never knew their species.
        Don't know now. We're grown. Old.
        They're gone.

        Even with coal-burning furnace,
      two fireplaces, blue-flamed oven,
storm windows contemplating the gray, slow approach of snow,
      that house was cold.
Only this room simmered, ember-warm
      for heat rises, anger floats, snow burns
        like red-slapped, face-chapped skin—
          glows when sun strikes it
           just so—

Reptile

Curled on the floor, a snake: small, maybe a baby.
I rummage the kitchen of this house I barely know, find
a plastic container, round like for a cake, slap it on top
of the snake. He slithers to escape. Rattles. A rattlesnake!

Caged. Smug that I have him, I forget: he has me, too. I can't
lift the lid I put in place. No way to un-hem him. I plop a rock on top,
find cardboard, slide it under the container. Shaking, I flip it over. Seal it
with duct tape. Toss this latest mess into the woods, snake rattling away.

When David hears, he demands to see. I point. He traipses in, retrieves
the contraption. Curses. Untapes it, slaps the plastic face down in the dirt.
Lifts my cage, lets the snake zig away. *Trapped, vacuumed, thrashing
about—*
David shakes his head. *I couldn't leave him to him die like that. Could
you?*

But I could. I did. And he knew.

Forty Stories

I cut my teeth on *Vertigo:* Kim Novak thrown forty storeys—
blonde-coiffed, ivory swing coat askew, ice eyes orgasmic

ecstatic, not that wet spot on the pavement, understated.
I am at the center somewhere high not famous,

not the Eiffel, nor the Empire State, not even Sears Tower
but a building in Dallas, brick edifice, name obscured

down old Industrial Road, rechristened Riverfront,
somewhere a sniper stood for sure. No Kim Novak,

I reek, slovenly, eyes whiskey-leaking, noisy-crying
Ain't worth shooting someone said. Another B-movie

etched in my psyche, black gone white, just static buzz.
And fetal at center, spun by the sky, sick with the sway,

I'm certain if I inch to the edge, this man in that suit
(skinny tie, smooth line) wants to show me the view.

Tossed off, thrown over, I am that scrap of paper
scribbled with something you need to remember:

a to-do list, recipe, important number, maybe,
for whom you forget.

Bloodletting: Requiem for Amy Winehouse

Another urban legend implodes,
shards of her mind sizzling like fireflies
behind tired eyes—

This, the girl with spiders in her hair,
bee-hive abuzz, brain going, going
gone when the shellac, at last, cracks.

Her tattooed wish-list nailed to our doors
(I'm ugly, fuck you, love me), her fishnet
fragility implores us question our answers:

Who gets to be soft and pretty? Is pain petty?
We, too, cried with you on the kitchen floor
and cheated ourselves, like you knew we would.

As for me, I hope her headstone reads,
What kind of fuckery is this?
Who knew those 45s get stuck? Incessant track:

the hole in your coat you can't leave alone,
those poems you write over and over again,
the places we cut so that nothing is whole—

for cleanliness lies next to godlessness.
We all go back to black, Amy, just not as soon
as you, and most neither publicly nor bravely.

Broke

I remember the day we took that picture:
me in a Goodwill muslin dress, size five,
pushing a stroller; Blythe, the baby,
looking pouty; Dominique in a bow
as big as her head; Genevieve smirking,
eating ice cream. We're at Heights festival
holding balloons (a splurge since we were poor).
We let go of them later.

I remember the day I broke that picture,
smashed the frame across the coffee table
covered with papers and clutter and dirt—
TV blaring, kids screaming, me drinking
five-dollar wine. I cut my hand on the glass.
Now I wish I could get it back—that picture.
I don't even have the negative.

After Winter

We threw the sheets in the dumpster—
tubes and bottles and catheters.
I found that dress with the flowers—
cleaned you, dressed you, buried
my face in your hair.

I just wanted you to be clean

We opened all the doors, and the cold
February wind whipped the curtains
blew that picture off the wall—
cherry blossoms and Mt. Fuji snow,
stark like your fury, white like goodbye.

We were never quite housekeepers, you and I—

Tennessee farm folk, picking strawberries,
walking our stories, eating the basil we weeded,
planting seeds—Big Boy tomatoes, leeks, rutabaga,
licking homemade fudge with our fingers—
ever busy, always dirty,
dirty as earth
with life.

Spring Clean

Bernice, I see you
and I call you,
fruit fallen not
far from the tree
of your blue kitchen
with white curtains
& the junk drawer. You
sport a sleeveless shift;
sort dimes, loose screws,
damp S&H Green Stamps,
needles rammed into spools
of lime green thread, unused,
box-tops you meant to send in
for something free you didn't need
and lids, lots, for lost Tupperware
bought because—

You give up. Dump the junk
across your clean table, Early
American Maple, Ethan Allen, no
less, bought when you got back
to the States, coins clinking a hole
in ex-pat pockets. But it didn't last,
went fast, on paint from Glidden
and a four-poster bed, no canopy—
Later, you said. But good went
bad. Poverty. Crumbs. Cliches:
It's all in your head and *Better
to have it & not need it...* Is it?

So poor, your parents never
dreamt to want more and
now I get what you got:
the hoard, a sideboard
where goods get pitched
just brimming with
verdant promise,
like stamps
already
licked.

Burnt Dust

1.

In a junk store, I sort through stacks of photos—
wedding pictures, black and white, orchids gone gray.
The bride chose that bouquet, picked the lace, those gloves,
the garden gate or trellis, backdrop for this most auspicious day.
What is this stuff? Who keeps keepsakes? Impulses lost, paper
translucent, names faded or forgot. I have heard that fires begin
in dust. Did you know dust can burn? Yes. Burn the house down.

2.

In ashes of burnt dust, I tally the number of lovers who have died
these past four years. Five. Faintly I remember sweat and secretions.
How one taught me about Mozart; one clipped his nails to the quick
(the better to feel you with, my dear), brayed like a dying wildebeast
in his over-heated bed. The third had never heard of Thomas Hobbes,
said the social contract wasn't really a thing. The next crushed my now-
frail bones beneath the weight of his need. The last swept me away—
no hurricane, just dust, with just as much disdain. Such fuss! I recall
their beds, stale sheets, me—my encouraging murmurs, words unsaid:
a little to the left, please. Where did all those juices flow when they died?
Which they did.

Other

Sharks feed if they smell blood.
They smell blood everywhere—
even a drop.

Shark babies devour each other
in the womb,
that other blood-bathed sea.

Sharks feed in the dark.
I am, you are
afraid. There are other things to fear:

being alone.

Everyone is born alone, gives birth
alone, suffers and dies alone,
groans with the grit of it.

I thought marriage, kids, work, friends
would make me less like that pebble
moon, more like an ocean—

not this

shark stalking, ranging far, questing for
one warm spot
of blood.

The Thing with Feathers

Swarms of pelicans storm the beach,
gather at the edge of the water. The wind
has scattered feathers all over. My daughter
gathers a bouquet, bone white, gray as the day.

She schemes to make a dream catcher.

You cannot take home every feather,
I tell her, no matter how light. Their weight
accumulates, suffocates, prevents flight.
Better to make a duster. Gather dust.

Dreams are tricky, fleeing things you can't
catch with webs, woven from what's fallen.
Try to sneak, hope for luck, work for food.
You can't spend sand—dollars, that is.

Now I'm remembering the lover I thought
would cost me nothing. No bread winner,
no. But he brought the butter, the sugar,
made mornings sweeter. Then, it was later

than I thought. High noon. Dark. Light had flown
like a flock of pelicans driving the edge of a storm.
See that baby shark? Washed up, Must've thought
he was going somewhere, swimmingly. Life flying by.

The poet was wrong. Hope is heavy.

Drop the feathers, I tell my daughter. Stop scavenging
the beach for baubles that turn to rubble. Cute becomes
clutter. You won't want it when you get home. I know.
Don't drag driftwood. Let it drift.

music before words

conduit of god

if i touch
your hem
if i kiss

your hand
bleeding a blue note

forgive
this

flawed daughter
fractured
mother

fickle lover
listener
only

holding holy water
in sieved hands
broken bowl

not gold
clay

as close to grace
as I come
this

still night

Poetry Remains

I saved your poems.

An indecent burial
might have been better
tossed to the compost
hauled to a shredder
pitched with kitty litter
fodder and filler—

Catharsis in a cat box.

Maybe you gave me
a wake, wished away
my lint on your memory
dust on the spectacles
you couldn't find.
Perhaps you said
sometimes good goes bad
life runs awry.

Still, poetry remains.

Your poems are safe with me
keeper of clutter and lovers and dreams
They're the hair I burn in my candle
the cord buried under my tree.
Your offerings   my longings   this shrine—
I saved them. I made them mine.

A Real Dive

What is Wild?

How to praise what is wild, coming as I do from a land
where fences sprout like weeds only white, tumbling rock
walls built by men who just wanted work?

How to praise what is wild, writing from my own
Great Depression? I remember my mother's garden,
pruned and weeded, seedlings in vermiculite, fertilized
in silent spring, chemicals that killed her with cancer.

I think of the terra cotta tiles, tiny footprints
from unknown critters who skittered across clay—
how lucky were they never to have known that house
on Sage Canyon, the one that became a prison.

My first abode was wood, second asbestos,
third cinderblock, fourth aluminum siding, fifth brick,
I lose track. All those walls.

I come from the Good Book, practical shoes, Original Sin, grits.
In this city of unfettered color and cobblestones, I step carefully,
barely brave enough to take a city bus. This, my fifth trip to Mexico.

My parents drove our 64 Dodge Dart to Mexico City when I was six.
I remember wild horses running down the mountainside. How Dad
stopped the car to whip me for whining about some scribble-scrabble
in my coloring book. Outside the lines. That was something.

The horses, I mean.

American Ugly

It has come to this: I am paying someone to touch me.
I trudge up Calle Canal in the ruthless sun for one of five
massages I bought in bulk. *Quanto cuesta?* 1700 pesos,
$100 American dollars, $20 a pop. In Bali it was five bucks
for a whole-body massage, $1 for feet. God, it felt good
after shopping for sarongs on sooty streets. But I got a guy
with pointy nails that one time. Got me thinking, *Yep, Hep C.*
We got to be careful. Stick to Cerveza. Don't eat green.

My masseuse is Dolores. I've only asked her name twice.
I should remember since it sounds like *dolares,* my one
speed bump now that I'm in San Miguel. It's not as cheap
as the rest of Mexico. The *touristas* are ruining it for the rest
of us *touristas.* As for the smug ex-pats, well, they make bank,
can buy agave juice for what ails them. Dolores seems clean
enough, and strong, how she moves her hands along my spine,
does that crazy figure-eight across my butt. Not bad for 20 bucks.

They say we store anger in our hips. Must be what ails me.
I'm good and pissed. But Dolores, she moves her hands just right
along the places trussed too tight, listens to me say *mas* or *menos.*
It's almost like love, as close as I come. In this city, the colors tumble
me off my feet and back on. But late afternoon, I walk off alone, down
another buck, another block. Hills to trudge, pretty piles of rocks. Fuck.
Looks like I had to tip, after all. Yeah, this is love. Conditional.

In Ireland

He said it won't be summer unless we go to Ireland
the coast, I suppose—Kerry County or the Hebrides—
Don't ask me how I know.

I picture the wind whipping my beer
afroth in a plastic cup. We take refuge in a pub,
get chummy over mugs of ale with some florid
ginger-haired clan, singing *You take the high road,*
over fish and chips or potatoes, boiled, hearty fare,
yes, trilling away the hours (*tura-lura-lura*) while a fire
outroars the storm.

Ireland boasts a poet in every pub,
sloppy with whiskey—that would be me.
And in this tea-cozy fantasy, we've quite forgotten
the dull chill of cold wind in what was meant to be
summer abroad on a sun-splashed coast
of Kerry County or the Hebrides.

Trickling Down

Sophisticated women are skinny,
got $500 boots and Gucci-ass pants,
arched eyebrows and concerned looks,
no shadow of a mustache, veins intact,
caramel hair, peaches in their cheeks,
the natural beauty that defies nature.

They own kilns, sell pottery to end poverty,
read the latest Zadie Smith, empathize
with biracial women like Zadie's big girls,
whose unruly follicles resist beauty parlor
torture, genes busting out their jeans—
they know what curvy fit really means.

Sophisticated women are never hungry
They have a glass of wine, watch the sun
glint off Puget Sound, or Santa Monica,
or some such place I might just visit but
will not stay, convinced the waiter sneered
or just rolled his eyes and sighed when I said,

I like my martini extra dirty, if you please.
And, no, I'll forego the escargot—I mean,
if it's an acquired taste, why bother? I always say,
to anyone listening, anyway. No one is. That's what
I get for getting fat or saying *supposably* or being born
on the puny side of the Big Dog tracks, or being born
at all, how's that?

Makes me want to shoplift salmon, eat hummus
with my hands, blow my nose on this linen napkin,
leave it for the snooty waiter to carry off in a bus pan.
That's what he gets.

Reflections: In the Rienzi

They announce their presence, these mirrors.
They will not catch you rounding a corner
scarfing a donut, looking demented, gray,
slovenly, old. They will not frame you
in bad light, huddled in a dressing room
on the cusp of summer—swimsuit season—
mumbling invocations, dreading the unveiling,
on the pale.

Narcissus did not need dolphins for fortune,
bees for industry, horns of plenty. He liked himself
well enough, with just a winning grin, water, clarity.
Most folks could use some help. You thought these ornate
mirrors would not flatter you. Not fatten you like a funhouse
image exactly, but drab you down, weighed and found wanting,
wan by comparison—size fourteen, hair too thin, face undone—
but it seems you look good in gilt, glowing even, awash in nuance.

In the Rienzi, every room a framed fantasy, these twin mirrors are
his-n-her replicas. No need ask a spouse about the size of your tiara,
or which mustache, handlebar or Hitler. Why even look at each other?
Consult this mirror:
Validation, affirmation, it-glitters-so-it-must-be-gold—a fleeting fallacy—
even decrepit old Zeus can get the girl if he wears the right outfit.
When the guided tour moves on, you find yourself lingering, alone
in the Italian room.

Drinking Bitters

The lure of the five-dollar glass of chianti,
plus olives, brie, and my five o'clock munchies,
make for unhappy hour at the Rainbow Lodge:

The terraced gardens, the eighties pop trio,
that wedding sweating the garden below,
I-do's limp as a blown-over rose,

another corsage left in the sun. I hate Kahlil Gibran,
hate every Sufi, anyone, really, who dances to ecstasy
including Lady GaGa, especially Madonna,

though I looked like her, blooming, once upon a corset,
or so I was told. She's still hot, thanks to mantras, yoga,
personal trainers, sex, and imbibing the blood of, like, a virgin.

Now, I might be sweaty, but hot? I'm not. Let the chianti breathe.
That's right. Breathe right through my pores. These flowers are wilting
like a worn-down libido. I should've ordered a dirty martini, Campari,

something bitter to beat the heat. I hate Texas. Hate happy couples.
Hate sitting under live oaks alone. This was a bad idea. I'm tipping
maybe ten percent. *Can you break a dollar?* I ask the waiter.

Someone bought your drinks, he says. Where? Over there. But the buyer
is gone, moved on, good deed done. My thighs are chafing; my heart,
a five-pound Faberge stone plunked in the Monet-look-alike pond

where the bride gazes, wistful,
fist full of lilies.

Have Another Hurricane

"They call it Stormy Monday. Tuesday's just as bad..."
T-Bone Walker

June, like a water balloon
got volleyed about until, thumb-
stuck and cumulous, she broke.

Dumped sultry blessings and sweat
on every summer wedding. Made mud
of my green yard. So, let's languish.

I mean, it's Houston, not Portland.
Some of us got SAD. We might need
to move to Phoenix or Tucson for sun.

Might need to go back to bed and
not get laid. Listen to our good friend's
bad CD, bought for 20 bucks at a blues jam.

We're a blues town, after all. Just ask
Muddy Waters. Drink the ennui away. Say
to the rain, *Make it stop*. Ask the wrong person

the right question. Remember James Dean
in *Giant* getting sloshed while the latest typhoon
threw buckets at the Shamrock Hotel. That big pool

I never swam in, but heard-tell from friends of an age
to have cocktailed there with River Oaks Aunt Sybil,
maraschino cherries in bottomless Shirley Temples.

James Dean in that flick could never shake the dust
out from under his nails. His poor wife. Unlike Rock
Hudson, old-monied, remember? How he stood up

for brown folks in diners. Stellar. *Giant* starts in Marfa,
where dust gives way to art these days. At the Paisano,
we stay in the Dennis Hopper suite. Good food. Try the flan.

Drink up.

Sea

White girls on this khaki beach
drink wine with names they can't pronounce,
tote bland blonde babies and buckets blue,
accessorize bikinis in shades of chartreuse,
(sans cellulite, veins intact, tan lines undefined)
sport husbands with Visas and paunches and Porsches,
ignore or adore them, it's all the same—
the stories they tell:

If he buys me lingerie again
I'll scream. I mean
teddies, garters, bustiers—as if—

You don't need no fancy panties,
don't need no corkscrews.
You are fat, wear black, in fact,
you border on insane,
glower at that Lexus double-parked,
those pretty babes, their pretty babies
lawn chairs from Academy,
umbrellas, frisbees,
strawberries, brie.
Listen:
children whine
it's mine it's mine it's mine

Who owns this sand?
you wonder
hot, sunburned, bored—
chug some warm R.C.
put down your tattered koozie,
take off your dime store shades,
look past whitecaps, sandbars, seabirds, sea
to the place where blues collide
seamless and immense.

It's About Time

after Mary Oliver's "Wild Geese"

You do not have to write a poem.
You do not have to sew a quilt, paint egrets,
lose fifty pounds, eat right, meditate.

You only have to listen for the rhythm
of this present: the songs of birds
and sounds of work,
folks hammering, hollering, building
what is left to be built.

Tell me about the children on your block
drawing rainbows on the street with sidewalk chalk.
Meanwhile there are masks to be made and worn.
Meanwhile kids are riding scooters in streamers of pink
and mothers and fathers are reigning them in
or urging them on or emptying bedpans or watering lawns
or drinking wine as afternoon wains.

Whoever you are, life calls you to love the breath of each season,
the breathing that comes easy as opium filling your willing lungs,
the inhale before the song you sing when no one is listening,
or even the rough, raspy suck of an uphill ride on a rusty bike
announcing that time is all any of us has
every breath-blessed day.

Multnomah Summer

Tell me, have you ever pined
for light? Like dreaming of a lover,
naked under white sheets
long, longing afternoons
spent
watching sun wain,
waiting for night—
Do you remember?
And when you close your eyes, find
kaleidoscopes on fire.

Me, I pine for light, even now,
eyes shaded against the glare.
When that late-day glint
hits my wine just right,
I can taste it:
sun swelling and spilling
from grapes a girl danced to froth—
bare feet, gold throat, farmer's arms—
cinematic like a movie classic.

Then from Arles to Portland
every flower opens. Such honey!
Purple thistle, rose, goldenrod.
Sunflowers for a blue room.
Queen's Lace. Lavender ice.
Mount Hood, a snow cone
in the sun.

So, linger longer. Know full well
we'll wait late for that last train,
huddled, night blind, cold
save for this warmth:
plucked tender from summer
planted young in our blood
watered by eyes closed tight
clasped in old hands, stiff
yet sticky with glut. Want.
All that light.

What the Sun Said: Kerrville Folk Festival, day 18

On Chapel Hill the Sun opened
his one good eye. It landed on 30
dirty hippies greeting sunrise in song,
thrumming, "We're the last ones left."
It was Jena alone he sought—she,
wrapped in ragged faux fur coat,
thin knees peeking out holey tights,
arms draped about Chris Chandler,
poet of dust mites and the divine.

"Jena," the Sun said. "We are far away
from Frank O'Hara's NYC. Our hill country
is a lot warmer than Russia. Chances are
Vladimir Mayakovski would not have fared
well in Texas heat, quaffing tequila, not vodka.
Both may have stayed inside in the AC,
never conversed with me. Orpheus might
have preferred to brave Hades rather than
drag Euridice up to hot caliche dust,
windblown, like the answers you seek.

But each morning I see you with the *I Ching*.
Its words beckon the poem, the poem
that speaks to your prayer: Make it right.
The sorrow that burns behind your eyes
seers mine. I am here to tell you I see you.
I, too, rise each day I want to die. You say
Poetry heals, and I hear *Get up. Get up.*
Throw your arms around us. So I rise,
cast this light for your sake and mine.

Believe me, Jena, I see some shit.
We all are broken, nothing left but this
to wrap our wounds: love, a holy coat.
I am glad you wait with raised hands.
open eyes. Good's to be had from bad.
Believe you me, I bless the Devil's Backbone,
the crooked and the straight. My road is broad,
not narrow. Wait for light. Stand. Wait.

The Weight of Smoke

My daughter does yoga at the end the dock.
The sun, a sliver of apricot, serpentines the lake.
Toward or away? It is hard to say. The sky's a haze
but for that one wayward slice of sun. The place
where water and sky meet is indistinct as anxiety,
and now there is only gray. Which daughter
slices the water on her long board like the old man
in the sampan of a Chinese painting? Hard to say.

We know what appears to be fog is smoke. The woods
are on fire, have been burning for days. The ash floats.
It makes the lake so lovely we almost forget to be upset,
neglect to remember the state of the planet, fires within
and without filtering the late-day light. My daughter,
hands upraised, salutes the sun. Both go down.

Still stumps of trees waver, submerged in water.
I look for them in early morning clarity, miss them.
Come afternoon, find only shadows blue and diffused.
Is it enough to know the trees are there, what is left
at least? Everything has something beneath.

What we see—when we see—is light.
It bends, reflects, vibrates off the lake, these trees,
ash and embers, sons and daughters, each other,
one another—everything.
Everything is light.

Birthday

In Tulum, the cenotes are holy,
pock marks of long-fallen stars

the coldest blue, swaddling stones
so old—

Here, I can
believe, almost,

I am beautiful.
Unoriginal sins clean gone

I dive, glide, float—
grateful

to my mother for my birth,
her laugh

to my father who taught me to swim,
arms and breath in tandem

to daughters who ushered me to this space
to friends slogging through the sacred cave

of a poem penned quickly, maybe badly,
transcribed by hand—

the right one, belonging
to a body

I strive to love
with the same tenacity

as it loves me.

Traveling Light

Shells spatter the beach in morning sun.
January, the god with two faces, looks
fore and aft, and I forgo collecting more
baubles that crumble until I toss them
in the dumpster with last night's leftovers.

For some shells have live things hiding inside
that die a little sooner away from the water—
more karma in a cache already over packed,
remnants of remnants stored in plastic bins
which will endure even after the Apocalypse
that must surely ensue. More rubble to ponder.

No, I have no interest in shells this scattered day.
My brain bubbles and babbles, cauldron-full.
I look over the water, not quite a sheet of light,
waves roving to and fro, and see that it is good—
and my pockets will be empty when I go.

Laundromat

Used to be I took my poems out in public
wearing stretch pants and puffy pink curlers.
Look, folks said, offended. *We, too, have suffered.*

This is the place where the poems come tumbling
out of that pit they've been in all winter.

This is the day I say to joy, *Marry me.* Drag her
kicking and squealing over the threshold.

Come on. Come in. Come home.

Praise for *The Hungry Ghost Diner*

Ellis's subject matter is as variegated and extensive as the poet's prodigious knowledge. A master of paradox, she artfully conveys both the coldness of philosophical reflection and the scalding heat of human passion, often within the confines of a single poem. The range of her allusions, always spot-on, is nothing less than stunning. In "The Stuff They Feed Us" alone, she references Enkidu, Persephone, Eve, God, Satan, Socrates, Buddha, Kafka, Wonder Bread, Kool-Aid and Christ. Ellis's ekphrastic poems are especially noteworthy and skillfully executed, triggered by a range of artists from The Mangbetu to Salvador Dalí and Botticelli to Courbet.

Ellis's assured and direct poetic diction, at its best, brings to mind that of Plath, especially the latter's boldness in pushing assonance and alliteration to the edge of the abyss while never allowing it to plunge into monotonous oblivion. Such linguistic skill is evident throughout Ellis's collection, exemplified by the following: "Not one to be caught off guard / I kill us off out of habit"; and "Dead flesh is made succulent / by marinating, braising, pounding— / broken down to please the palate."

This reviewer gives The Hungry Ghost Diner *his highest recommendation.*

—Larry D. Thomas, 2008 Texas Poet Laureate

From its title through to its final poem, Kelly Ann Ellis's The Hungry Ghost Diner is a marvel of deeply textured and beautifully paradoxical ideas, arisings, and relationships. In a voice so equally authoritative and self-deprecating that it can only be the voice of wisdom, and in a style both skillfully crafted and as easily flowing as a coffee refill at a diner, Ellis blends elevated intellectual and cultural references with a working-class intelligence and sensibility to examine the joys and difficulties of aging, interpersonal relationships, class dynamics, poverty, and other such vital topics. Ultimately, through her sophisticated literary prowess, Ellis imbues her subject matter with the kind of warm humor and vibrant conversational detail that make a reader wish she could stay at The Hungry Ghost Diner forever, conversing deep into the night with this soulful, generous poet.

–Melissa Studdard, author of *Dear Selection Committee* and *I Ate the Cosmos for Breakfast*